COMPREHENSION

TO 14

ANSWER BOOK

KIM RICHARDSON

Consultant Editor: Geoff Barton

OXFORD
UNIVERSITY PRESS

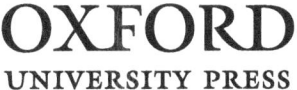

UNIVERSITY PRESS

Great Clarendon Street, Oxford OX2 6DP

Oxford University Press is a department of the University of Oxford.
It furthers the University's objective of excellence in research,
scholarship, and education by publishing worldwide in

Oxford New York

Auckland Cape Town Dar es Salaam Hong Kong Karachi
Kuala Lumpur Madrid Melbourne Mexico City Nairobi
New Delhi Shanghai Taipei Toronto

With offices in

Argentina Austria Brazil Chile Czech Republic France Greece
Guatemala Hungary Italy Japan Poland Portugal Singapore
South Korea Switzerland Thailand Turkey Ukraine Vietnam

Oxford is a registered trade mark of Oxford University Press
in the UK and in certain other countries

© Oxford University Press 2012

Database right Oxford University Press (maker)

First published 1997; this new edition published 2012

All rights reserved. No part of this publication may be reproduced,
stored in a retrieval system, or transmitted, in any form or by any means,
without the prior permission in writing of Oxford University Press, or as
expressly permitted by law, or under terms agreed with the appropriate
reprographics rights organization. Enquiries concerning reproduction
outside the scope of the above should be sent to the Rights Department,
Oxford University Press, at the address above

You must not circulate this book in any other binding or cover and you
must impose this same condition on any acquirer

British Library Cataloguing in Publication Data

Data available

ISBN 978-0-19-832110-1

10 9

Typeset in India by TNQ

Printed in Great Britain by Ashford Print and Publishing Services,
Gosport

Contents

Introduction — 5

Challenge Level 1

Unit 1:	1.1 Finding Your Way in London	6
Unit 2:	1.2 Chutney Gift Crisis	9
Unit 3:	1.3 Let's Do Pizza!	11
Unit 4:	1.4 Starting a Band	13
Unit 5:	1.5 Very Short Stories	15
Unit 6:	1.6 Chocoholics Beware!	17

Challenge Level 2

Unit 1:	2.1 Being a Kitesurfer	19
Unit 2:	2.2 Teachers: I Love You!	21
Unit 3:	2.3 Letters to Myself	23
Unit 4:	2.4 Surf's Up!	26
Unit 5:	2.5 Treason!	28
Unit 6:	2.6 Pet Care	30

Challenge Level 3

Unit 1:	3.1 Make 'em Win!	34
Unit 2:	3.2 Attack of the Killer Bees!	36
Unit 3:	3.3 Quacking Ducks and Icebergs!	38
Unit 4:	3.4 Work Experience? No, Thanks!	40
Unit 5:	3.5 Heading to a New School	42

CONTENTS

Challenge Level 4

Unit 1:	4.1 I Fell 6000 Feet and Survived!	44
Unit 2:	4.2 The Meat We Eat	46
Unit 3:	4.3 Putting the Boot into Skiing	48
Unit 4:	4.4 My Pet Human	50

Challenge Level 5

Unit 1:	5.1 Genius or Mad Man?	52
Unit 2:	5.2 Badger Watch	54
Unit 3:	5.3 The Day the Earth Shook	56
Unit 4:	5.4 Iceberg!	58

Introduction

Welcome to our all-new edition of *Comprehension to 14*. Published almost 15 years ago, the original book was a big hit with students and teachers because they liked its clarity of purpose and its no-nonsense approach. Some even liked its cover!

The new Student Book and Answer Book have been rewritten from scratch and reflect the work I have been doing in recent years as a teacher and head teacher, as well as a consultant to a number of Government agencies. This new experience has given me a strong sense that it's time for us to rev up the way we teach reading in secondary schools.

At Key Stage 3, traditionally we have tended to 'do' reading. That is, we have placed texts in front of students and expected them to read and understand them. The evidence suggests that increasingly we need to be doing more than simply 'doing' reading: we need to teach reading skills much more explicitly.

That's why we have so radically reconceptualised *Comprehension to 14*. It's now not simply a collection of texts for students to read and respond to. It's a book that is designed to do nothing less than help them to become better readers. It takes the literacy skills that we as adults employ day in and day out, often unconsciously, and it helps students – whatever their backgrounds or abilities – to learn to do the same.

This new Answer Book includes both questions and sample answers for most of the activities in the Student Book (although questions which ask for personal judgement have not been included). With these, we are not of course suggesting that only one answer will fit, but experience tells us that students need to learn that in English it's about **how** we express our ideas as well as **what** we say. The sample answers are designed to help nudge students towards an appropriate style. I hope you will find them helpful and that the suggested answers will speed up your own evaluation of your students' progress.

Geoff Barton
Consultant Editor

Challenge Level 1: Unit 1

1.1 Finding Your Way in London

Basic reading skills (page 12)

1 **Find a station which has disabled access from the street to the platform.**

   Sample answers:
   - Canada Water
   - Stratford
   - Kilburn
   - Oakwood
   - Westminster
   - Richmond

2 **Find a station which has a riverboat icon.**

   Sample answers:
   - Westminster
   - Waterloo
   - London Bridge
   - Cutty Sark for Maritime Greenwich
   - North Greenwich (for the O_2)

3 **Write down two stations that are either side of Oxford Circus.**

   Sample answers:

   On the Central line: Bond Street and Tottenham Court Road

   On the Bakerloo line: Regent's Park and Piccadilly Circus

   On the Victoria line: Green Park and Warren Street

4 **Write down the two stations that are either side of East Putney.**

   Putney Bridge and Southfields

5 **Which station is the next station heading east from South Kensington?**

   Sloane Square

6 **Which station is the next station heading west from Mile End?**

   Bethnal Green

7 **Look at the green District line and answer the following questions:**

   a) **Name the station which is the furthest south.**

   Wimbledon

   b) **Name the station which is furthest east.**

   Upminster

   c) **True or false: Charing Cross is on the District line?**

   False

CHALLENGE LEVEL 1 UNIT 1

8 Look at the information at the bottom of the map about the different line names and answer the following questions:

a) True or false: the Hammersmith & City line is green?

False

b) True or false: the Circle line is yellow?

True

c) True or false: there is a Buckingham line?

False

9 a) Find two instances on the map where an aeroplane icon appears.

Sample answers:
- Heathrow Terminals 1, 2, 3
- Heathrow Terminal 4
- Heathrow Terminal 5
- London City Airport

b) What do you think this icon means?

These underground stations serve an airport.

10 How many interchange stations are there on the Central line?

14

11 How many stations on the Circle line have step-free access?

4

Advanced reading skills (page 12)

1 Write the stations you would go through if you were travelling from Tottenham Court Road (page 10) to:

a) Waterloo

Leicester Square, Charing Cross, Embankment, Waterloo

b) Marylebone

Oxford Circus, Regent's Park, Baker Street, Marylebone

c) Notting Hill Gate.

Oxford Circus, Bond Street, Marble Arch, Lancaster Gate, Queensway, Notting Hill Gate

2 Write down the name of the station that you would change at if you were travelling from Oxford Circus (page 10) to:

a) Knightsbridge

Green Park (for the Piccadilly line)

b) Kensington (Olympia)

Victoria (for the District line)

c) Stamford Brook.

Victoria (for the District line)

CHALLENGE LEVEL 1 UNIT 1

3 Which would be the route with the fewest changes from Piccadilly Circus (page 10) to:

a) **Lancaster Gate**

Take the Bakerloo line north from Piccadilly Circus to Oxford Circus. Change here for the Central line. Take the Central line west three stops and you will arrive at Lancaster Gate.

b) **High Street Kensington**

Take the Bakerloo line south two stops and change to the Circle or District line. Take the Circle or District line west seven stops and you will arrive at High Street Kensington.

Alternatively, you can take the Piccadilly line from Piccadilly Circus west four stops. Change for the Circle or District line at South Kensington. Take this line two stops north and you will arrive at High Street Kensington.

c) **Putney Bridge?**

Take the Bakerloo line south from Piccadilly Circus two stops to Embankment. Change at Embankment and take the District line west for 11 stops to Putney Bridge.

Alternatively, take the Piccadilly line from Piccadilly Circus west four stops to South Kensington (or six stops to Earl's Court). Change at South Kensington (or Earl's Court) for the District line. Take the District line west for six stops to Putney Bridge.

Early Bird: Word generator (page 13)

How many words can you create from the letters in 'underground'?

Sample answers:

doe, dud, duo, due, den, end, god, nod, odd, one, our, red, run, rug, dude, dune, done, euro, gone, goer, noun, nerd, ogre, rude, dodge, nudge, order, roger, rogue, udder, droned, drudge, ground, gunner, runner, undone, dungeon, rounded, rounder, undergo, grounded

Challenge Level 1: Unit 2

1.2 Chutney Gift Crisis

Basic reading skills (page 16)

Skimming:

1 What do you think is the main aim of the website? Is it to get you to buy the items for sale, to show you how to make chutneys, to give you information about what the products contain or to tell you the price of the products on the site?

To get you to buy the items for sale

2 Who do you think has written the text on the website?

Sarah Fraser

3 How can you tell that the company selling the preserves is a small one?

Sample answer:

Cheques are to be made payable to an individual person within the company, Sarah Fraser.

Scanning:

1 Which is the sweetest type of product: chutneys, relishes or pickles?

Chutneys

2 True or false: the relish is sharp?

True

3 True or false: all three products contain vinegar?

True

4 True or false: the text was definitely written by Sarah Fraser?

False

5 How many products weigh 280 grams?

Five

6 Which product comes in the largest size?

Cranberry Chutney, 900 grams

7 How many products cost £3.00?

One: Cranberry Chutney, 280 grams

Advanced reading skills (page 16)

1 What does the writer mean when she says one product has a 'more awake' flavour?

The addition of the orange makes it a sharper taste.

2 What is the effect of using an exclamation mark at the end of paragraph one?

Sample answer:

The exclamation mark makes it seem as if the writer is enthusiastic about the product. It also makes it seem as if the writer is speaking directly to the reader.

CHALLENGE LEVEL 1 UNIT 2

3 True or false: the writer is correct to use a capital letter for 'Vegetarian'?

False. Grammatically, the capital letter is not necessary but the writer may have used it to draw attention to this feature of the product.

4 What is 'game' in 'game pies'?

Wild animals, including birds that are hunted, such as pheasant

5 What do you think turmeric is? Is it a spice, a type of fruit or a chemical?

It is a spice.

Numeracy:

1 How much would you spend if you ordered three jars of apple and mint relish, two jars of brinjal pickle and one jar of corn relish?

£15

2 If you have £40 to spend and need to buy two large cranberry chutneys, what is the maximum number of other products that you could buy?

Nine

3 If you bought one of each product, what would be their combined weight?

3.385 kilograms

Early Bird: Riddle (page 17)

> **Can you solve this riddle? 'Take off my skin and I won't cry, but you will. What am I?'**
> An onion

Challenge Level 1: Unit 3

1.3 Let's Do Pizza!

Basic reading skills (page 20)

1 How many different pizzas are on the menu?
Five

2 How many different types of pasta dish are on the menu?
Four

3 True or false: the menu tells you a bit about the history of the restaurant?
True

4 How many dishes are suitable for vegetarians?
Six

5 Which pizza is topped with artichokes?
Pizza Vegetariana

6 Which pasta contains aubergine?
Melanzane Parmigiana

7 Which pizza contains chicken?
Pizza Pollo

8 How many dishes contain parmesan?
Two

Advanced reading skills (page 20)

1 What is the Italian for 'four cheeses'?
Quattro Formaggi

2 What is the Italian for 'vegetarian'?
Vegetariana

3 Your friend likes cherry tomatoes but does not like pesto. Which pizza should he or she not order?
Pomodoro Special

4 Your other friend doesn't fancy pizza but doesn't quite fancy pasta. What would you recommend from the menu?
Melanzane Parmigiana

5 Your group orders: one Pomodoro Special, one Pizza Vegetariana, two Cannelloni and one Lasagna. How much does it cost?
£43

6 How does the menu make you think that the restaurant has a high quality of cooking?

Sample answers:
- The dishes are described in detail, mentioning high-quality ingredients and often using Italian terms and lots of adjectives.
- The prices are quite high.

CHALLENGE LEVEL 1 UNIT 3

7 Name one thing you like about the layout of the menu.

Sample answers:

- The design: use of colours and images
- Clear separation of the dishes under two headings – pizza and pasta – which makes finding information easier

Early Bird: Word generator (page 21)

How many words can you create from the letters in 'cannelloni'?

Sample answers:

ale, ice, inn, oil, one, acne, call, cell, coil, cola, lace, lane, lion, nail, nine, once, alone, canoe, canon, cello, clean, linen, ocean, canine, cannon, lanolin

Challenge Level 1: Unit 4

1.4 Starting a Band

Basic reading skills (page 26)

1 **Look more closely at the scene the writer describes in the first paragraph. Choose two details that make it seem like an ugly and unpleasant landscape.**

   Sample answer:
   - The weather is poor: it is freezing and about to rain.
   - The area is made of concrete and badly maintained, including a dribbling fountain, litter and a broken clock.

2 **The writer describes the scene near the library. Draw a sketch showing what you think it looks like, labelling some of the different characters and groups that are present.**

   Students should have drawn a sketch that includes some, or all, of the following features: library steps, McDonald's restaurant, fountain, museum tower with a broken clock, Liam, CJ, Daz, Gemma and her friends, girls carrying designer bags, families, elderly couples, Goths, Kevs and skaters.

3 **The writer writes that 'CJ was having a heavy conversation' with Gemma. Write down what you think 'heavy' means in this context.**

   Sample answer:

   Serious

4 **The writer says that the weather 'didn't want to commit itself'. Which of these words best describes what he means: 'moody', 'changeable', 'mixed' or 'unpredictable'?**

   Changeable

5 **What sparks the narrator's interest in starting a band?**

   A thought that pops into his head out of nowhere

6 **What instrument did Liam (the narrator) play at one stage in his life?**

   The recorder

CHALLENGE LEVEL 1 UNIT 4

Advanced reading skills (page 26)

1 **Look at the character of the narrator. What impression do we get of him from the story? Use a spider diagram to collect all the information you can about him from the text.**

Sample answer:

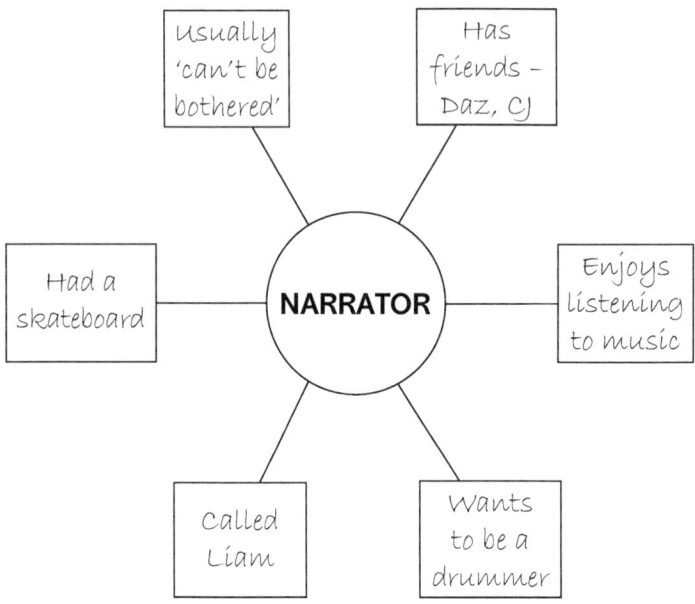

4 **The narrator describes the events of the weekend as strange. He says 'wheels were turning'. What do you think he means by this?**

Sample answer:

The narrator means that forces were at work that were bigger than himself, which would result in a major change, like the cogs on a machine turning in a mechanical product.

Early Bird: Riddle (page 27)

> **Can you solve this riddle? 'I have lots of keys but I can't open anything. What am I?'**
> A piano

Challenge Level 1: Unit 5

1.5 Very Short Stories

Basic reading skills (page 31)

Text A: 'Shattered Dreams and False Dawns'

1 How can you tell that the main character is feeling worried?

His heart is pounding and his chest is tight (physical symptoms of fear).

2 What do the words 'front line', 'missiles' and 'counter-attack' make you think of?

War or battle

3 As you first read this story, what did you guess the situation was?

Preparing for an enemy attack in battle

4 In a sentence, explain what this story is about.

A teacher is about to teach his class and is frightened of the noise and potential conflict.

Text B: 'There's No Place Like It'

1 What did you first think 'There's No Place Like It' was about?

Alien invasion

2 Who are the aliens in this story? How do you know?

The aliens are humans who embarked on space travel. We know this as they are described as 'human-looking' and they call Earth 'home'.

3 Which of the following descriptions best sums up the story: 'Earth is being invaded'; 'The President is confused'; or 'Some humans have been into space and are returning home'?

Some humans have been into space and are returning home.

4 What do you think the word 'universal' means in this story?

Travelling through the universe

Text C: 'Sharp Practice'

1 What did you think 'Sharp Practice' was going to be about when you started reading it?

Someone is about to kill or harm someone else with his knife.

2 In a sentence, summarize what this short story is about.

Someone is carving a roast chicken for five others to eat.

Advanced reading skills (page 32)

4 Compare the three stories and decide:

a) Which story uses the most difficult language?

Sample answer:

'Shattered Dreams and False Dawns' because it includes difficult vocabulary such as 'inevitable onslaught', 'crescendo' and 'futility'.

CHALLENGE LEVEL 1 UNIT 5

b) Which story has the biggest surprise at the end?

Sample answer:

'Sharp Practice', because the killer becomes just a cook carving a bird.

c) Which story is funniest?

Sample answer:

'Shattered Dreams and False Dawns' is the funniest because the writer compares the classroom to a war zone and suggests that the teacher is losing the battle.

5 Based on reading these three texts, what do you think are three essential ingredients in a good short story?

Sample answer:

Three essential ingredients to a good short story are: using powerful language, describing something that makes the reader puzzled or concerned and including a twist (a surprise).

Early Bird: Word generator (page 32)

How many words can you create from the letters in 'narrative'?

Sample answers:

ant, art, ear, eat, era, net, nit, ran, rat, tan, tie, tin, vat, van, area, earn, near, nave, neat, rain, rant, rave, rein, tear, tier, vein, vain, vine, arena, inert, raven, rivet, river, train, arrive, errant, retain, tavern, trainer

Challenge Level 1: Unit 6

1.6 Chocoholics Beware!

Basic reading skills (page 36)

1 **Name two companies that dominate the chocolate business.**

   Sample answers – choose two of:
   - Cadbury Schweppes
   - M&M/Mars
   - Hershey
   - Rowntree

2 **How much cocoa is produced each year?**

   Almost two million tonnes

3 **Where is the Ivory Coast?**

   West Africa

4 **How old were the children who were reported to be working without pay on farms?**

   From eight to twelve

5 **Which of these statements best explains what the Ivory Coast's Prime Minister says about child labour: 'Child labour is cheap and convenient'; 'Child labour happens because the companies don't pay farmers enough'; or 'Child labour is a bad thing'?**

   Child labour happens because the companies don't pay farmers enough.

6 **What does Ivory Coast's Prime Minister believe to be the solution to child labour?**

   Chocolate companies need to pay farmers a better price for cocoa.

Advanced reading skills (page 36)

1 **Look at one of the subheadings in the text: 'Bitter taste of the chocolate trade'. Explain what you think is meant by this.**

   It is referring to the negative side of chocolate production. The word 'bitter' has negative connotations and also cleverly links to the field of chocolate. This helps to show how unpleasant the idea of child labour is.

2 **Look at the ending of the article. Is it optimistic (positive) or pessimistic (negative) about the child labour situation? Explain your response.**

   Sample answer:

   It is optimistic because prices have returned to normal, and governments and chocolate companies have promised to work together. However, it is also pessimistic because it points out that child labour still exists.

CHALLENGE LEVEL 1 UNIT 6

5 The writer takes a quite complicated subject and aims to make it clear and straightforward for most readers. Copy the grid and make notes on the way that the writer tries to make the text accessible (easy to understand).

Sample answer:

FEATURE	HOW THE WRITER TRIES TO MAKE THE TEXT ACCESSIBLE
Layout (e.g. use of paragraphs, different font styles, use of images)	Four clear sections, three of which have a large image. The images are relevant to the text. Each section has a single paragraph. The second, third and fourth sections have subheadings in a green strip, reflecting the main heading of the article. A clear font is used, in a large point size.
Use of sentences (e.g. use of long and short sentences, use of questions as well as statements)	Most sentences are of average length, so you do not get lost in them. Sometimes there are shorter sentences for variety and impact, e.g. 'Today, chocolate is big business'. Most of the sentences are factual statements. One question is used, at the end of the introductory paragraph, which is answered by the information in the rest of the article.
Use of vocabulary (e.g. use of familiar or technical words, use of emotional or scientific words, amount of description)	Vocabulary is dominated by nouns, as this is factual writing rather than descriptive writing. There are a few adjectives, e.g. 'poor' and 'dangerous', referring to the conditions of work, but these are restrained rather than emotive. Formal language is used, e.g. 'nevertheless' and 'consume'. Some technical language is used, e.g. 'trafficked' and 'imports'.

Early Bird: Riddle (page 37)

> **Can you solve this riddle? 'What breaks and never falls and what falls and never breaks?'**
> Daybreak and nightfall

Challenge Level 2: Unit 1

2.1 Being a Kitesurfer

Basic reading skills (page 41)

1 When was Gisela Pulido born?

14th January 1994

2 What is her favourite television programme?

The Simpsons

3 In which years did she win the World Kitesurfing Championship?

2004 and 2005

4 What career ambition does Gisela have?

To become a vet

5 How old was Gisela when she began bodyboarding?

Three years old

6 Why did Gisela's family move to Tarifa?

To help Gisela become better at kitesurfing

7 As a result of moving to Tarifa, what two things helped Gisela to improve her kitesurfing?

It was windier than Barcelona and school ended at 2pm, which allowed her more time to practise.

8 Which was the most important year in her development as a kitesurfer: 2004 or 2005? Why?

Sample answer:

It was 2004, because she won the Kitesurfing World Championship for the first time.

Advanced reading skills (pages 41–42)

1 Look at the layout of the page. Write down three ways in which the designer tries to grab your interest.

Sample answers:

- Large, full colour, action photographs are used.
- A quotation describing Gisela's typical day is pulled out from the body of the text and appears in bold with a slightly larger font size.
- The text is colourful and bold.

4 Is the text aimed at people who are experts or general readers? Referring to the language used in the text, how can you tell?

Sample answer:

The text is aimed at general readers. There are no technical terms, and it is explained that Rip Curl and Da Kine are surf companies.

CHALLENGE LEVEL 2 UNIT 1

6 Notice how the writer ends some sentences in this text with exclamation marks (!). Which of these explanations do you think best explains why the writer uses these: 'The exclamation marks make the text more dramatic'; 'They make the style more informal'; 'They make the writer's attitude seem more positive'; 'They make the text look more interesting'; or 'They make it seem as if the writer is speaking the text, rather than writing'?

Sample answer:

They make the style more informal and they make it seem as if the writer is speaking the text, rather than writing it.

Early Bird: Word ladder (page 43)

> Changing just one letter at a time, get from the word RAIN to WIND in four steps.
> RAIN, RAID, RAND, WAND, WIND

Challenge Level 2: Unit 2

2.2 Teachers: I Love You!

Basic reading skills (page 47)

1. **Skim the text to get the gist of it: what is the writer saying he likes about teachers?**

   Sample answer:

   They unlock the potential in students.

2. **What job does Matt Damon's mother do?**

   She is a professor of early childhood education.

3. **Name the two places that Matt Damon flew from in order to attend the rally.**

   Vancouver and New York

4. **What type of schools did Matt Damon attend: public or private?**

   Public

5. **The writer lists five things that he values most about himself. Name two of them.**

   Sample answers – choose two of:

   - His imagination
   - His love of acting
   - His passion for writing
   - His love of learning
   - His curiosity

6. **What does he mean when he says: 'They were allowed to be teachers'?**

   He means that his teachers were not forced to do things like testing students, so they could spend their time and energy on effective teaching.

7. **What did Matt Damon's mother think that a standardized test would do to him?**

   She believed it would make him nervous.

8. **Matt Damon uses the phrase 'at the end of your rope'; what do you think he means?**

   Completely fed up and frustrated

9. **In the final paragraph, he says: 'the next time you're feeling down'. Write down another word meaning 'down' in the sense it is meant here.**

   Sample answers:

   Depressed, sad

10. **In the last sentence, he says: 'we will always have your back'. What do you think Matt Damon means by this?**

    He means 'we will always support you'.

CHALLENGE LEVEL 2 UNIT 2

Advanced reading skills (page 47)

1 Write down two ways you can tell that Matt Damon is passionate about the subject of his speech.

Sample answer:

- He travels a long way to deliver the speech.
- He lists five qualities that make him what he is, and attributes them to the kind of teaching he had.

2 What impression do you get of Matt Damon from his speech? Write down three words that you think describe him. Use examples from the text to support your choices.

Sample answer:

- Passionate ('incredible teachers'; 'we love you')
- Supportive ('there are millions of us behind you'; 'I think you're awesome')
- Thoughtful (imagining how he would have turned out if his teachers' job security had been based on his test results; 'as I get older, I appreciate…')

3 Write down two words to describe Matt Damon's mother. Then write a sentence explaining your choices.

Sample answer:

Clever and brave. She is clever because she's a professor of education; she is brave because she stands up for what she believes in and tells the school principal that a test is 'stupid'.

4 People who heard this speech were moved by it and were very grateful. Write down three ways in which Matt Damon makes the listeners feel good about themselves.

Sample answer:

- He tells them they are 'awesome'.
- He tells them that they are worth him travelling a long way to be with.
- He tells them that his key qualities are partly due to their work.

5 In the final paragraph, Matt Damon lists some of the criticisms of teachers. How does he show that these criticisms are wrong?

Sample answer:

He shows that teachers are not unappreciated and overpaid by stating that he and millions of others love them and support them.

Early Bird: Riddle (page 48)

> **Can you solve this riddle? 'The more you take, the more you leave behind. What am I?'**
> Footsteps

Challenge Level 2: Unit 3

2.3 Letters to Myself

Basic reading skills (page 52)

Text A: John Barrowman's letter

1 **Write down one piece of advice that the older John gives to his younger self.**

   Sample answers:
   - Dream big.
   - Work hard.
   - Floss every day.
   - Surround yourself with people who nurture your talents.
   - Buy shares in Apple.

2 **John Barrowman tells his younger self that there are no flying cars, hovercrafts and supersonic vehicles. Which of these statements best describes what he means: 'He is imagining what the future might be like'; 'He is saying that the future will not be as he has predicted'; 'He is saying that technology in the future is disappointing'; or 'He is saying that the future contains exciting transport'?**

   He is saying that the future will not be as he has predicted.

3 **What does the older John Barrowman tell the younger John Barrowman about what he will possess in the future?**

   Some 'really cool' cars

4 **What do you think he means at the end of his letter when he mentions the 'guys who invented an amazing piece of technology' and the company with a 'fruity name'?**

   He is referring to the invention of the Apple Macintosh personal computer.

Text B: Joanna Lumley's letter

1 **Write down one piece of advice that the older Joanna gives to her younger self.**

   Sample answers:
   - Do one thing at a time and do it properly.
   - Don't worry about spots.
   - Volunteer for everything.
   - Don't think you know everything.
   - Be daring.
   - Be polite.

2 **What does Joanna Lumley mean when she writes: 'Volunteer for everything because that way lies adventure'?**

   Sample answer:

   If you volunteer for things your life will be richer and more exciting because you will learn, experience, be challenged and stretched.

CHALLENGE LEVEL 2 UNIT 3

3 What do you think Joanna Lumley means by the phrase 'you have "attitude"'?

She means 'you are arrogant and rude'.

Advanced reading skills (pages 52–53)

1 Copy the grid below. Use it to compare the texts and explain what you notice about them.

Sample answer:

STATEMENT	AGREE OR DISAGREE?	REASON
John Barrowman's letter is more serious than Joanna Lumley's.	Disagree	Barrowman includes more jokes, e.g. about flossing and investing in Apple. Lumley is more thoughtful about the kinds of things that her younger self is doing and the problems she has.
John Barrowman's letter uses simpler language than Joanna Lumley's.	Disagree	Each writer uses quite simple language, except for 'nurture your talents' (Barrowman) and 'repellent' (Lumley).
John Barrowman seems to like his younger self more than Joanna Lumley likes hers.	Disagree	Barrowman's letter says very little about his feelings for his younger self: it is more about him now. Lumley has a lot of advice and some criticism for her younger self, but you can see that she is very fond of her ('thinking of you so much, you funny young person').

2 Which of the following words best describes John Barrowman's tone in his letter: 'happy'; 'optimistic'; 'angry'; 'uninterested'; or 'funny'? Choose the word and then write a sentence explaining why you think it fits the best.

Sample answer:

Funny, because he makes jokes about cars, his younger self watching *Dynasty*, flossing his teeth and missing out on a good investment.

3 Which of these words best describes the tone in which the older Joanna speaks to the younger one: 'cross'; 'affectionate'; 'angry'; 'warm'; or 'critical'? Choose the word and then write a sentence explaining why you think it fits the best.

Sample answer:

Affectionate, because she gives her younger self a lot of kind advice and has an understanding tone when she mentions her worst qualities.

CHALLENGE LEVEL 2 UNIT 3

4 Choose one quotation from each text that you think best demonstrates the attitude of the older writer to their younger self. Write a sentence explaining your choices.

Sample answer:

- 'Trust me' demonstrates Barrowman's attitude to his younger self because he thinks he knows more now than he did before.
- 'Be daring: be polite' demonstrates Lumley's attitude to her younger self because she mixes encouragement to push herself with advice to rein in her younger self's excesses.

Early Bird: Word ladder (page 53)

> **Changing just one letter at a time, get from the word COLD to the word WARM in four steps.**
>
> COLD, CORD, CARD, WARD, WARM

Challenge Level 2: Unit 4

2.4 Surf's Up!

Basic reading skills (page 56)

1 Tim Dowling doesn't give any names of who he is with in Cornwall. Some readers might find this confusing. Write down who the members of his family are and whether they are male or female.

- Tim Dowling – male
- His wife – female
- Eldest son – male
- Son's friend – male or female

2 Where is Tim Dowling's temporary office?

A patch of nettles on a hill

3 Tim Dowling's wife drives 'the three of us' up to the beach. Who are the three people?

Tim, his son and the son's friend

4 How can you tell that Tim Dowling doesn't really want to do any surfing?

Sample answer:

He considers saying he is too old so that 'it will get me out of surfing'. He is miserable in the car travelling to the beach. He says that his back hurts. He describes the experience in negative terms ('crowded', 'cold', 'exhausted').

5 How is Tim Dowling different from the other men in the group?

He is older and less able than they are.

6 When Tim Dowling finally gets into the water, what two things make it difficult for him to surf?

The currents are unpredictable and it is crowded.

7 What makes him fall off the board?

He tries to turn to avoid a girl crossing his path.

Advanced reading skills (page 57)

1 Write down three words which you think best describe the personality of Tim Dowling.

Sample answer:

Reserved, incompetent, unadventurous

2 Does Tim Dowling's family life seem happy? In a sentence, explain why or why not. Use an example from the text to support your answer.

Sample answer:

His family life seems happy because they do things together and talk together. For example, the son tries to persuade Tim to surf with his group further out at sea.

CHALLENGE LEVEL 2 UNIT 4

3 **Write down two features that make Tim Dowling's article different from other news stories you have read.**

Sample answer:

- It is based around the life of an ordinary family.
- It is amusing.

5 **Look at this sentence spoken by Tim Dowling's wife: 'Is Dad actually doing surfing?' What does the use of the word 'actually' tell us about her attitude?**

It tells us that she doesn't really believe that he wants to or is able to surf.

6 **Look at this sentence: 'Finally we are herded into the surf'.**

   a) What verb might the writer have used instead of 'herded'?

   Sample answers:

   Sent, driven, ordered, led, pushed, forced

   b) What effect does the choice of the word 'herded' have? What image does this word conjure in your mind?

   It suggests mass activity and unwillingness; the image is of a group of sheep or other animals that are being forced to move.

Early Bird: Word generator (page 58)

How many words can you create from the letters in 'surfboard'?
Sample answers:
ad, as, dab, bus, rub, rod, boar, bard, drab, fads, four, sour, ours, surf, ardour, broad, absurd, arbour, boards

Challenge Level 2: Unit 5

2.5 Treason!

Basic reading skills (page 63)

1 **Which of these sentences best summarizes what happens in the extract: 'There is a freak wave which kills William'; 'Two boys go too far into the sea and get stranded on some rocks'; 'Two boys fall into the sea and one of them drowns'; or 'A boy is lost at sea and his father keeps watch hoping for his return'?**

Two boys fall into the sea and one of them drowns.

2 **What is the name of the central character and what is his relationship to Matthew and Margery?**

William. He's the brother of Matthew and Margery.

3 **Write down two or three hints in the text that suggest it is not set in the modern day.**

Sample answers:

- The brothers reach the beach on horseback.
- There is a nurse, a servant and a stable boy.
- Will eats gruel from a wooden bowl and spoon.

4 **In the first paragraph, the writer says 'sand whipped into our faces'. What does the verb 'whipped' make you think of the way it felt?**

It stung their faces, as a whip would do.

5 **Look at paragraph two. Which word hints to the reader that the climb up the rocks is quite difficult?**

'Scrambled' or 'staggered'

6 **Which word best describes the father at the beginning of the extract: 'gloomy', 'mysterious', 'angry', 'frightened' or 'aggressive'? Write a sentence explaining your choice.**

Sample answers:

- The father is frightened, because he can see his sons are in danger.
- The father is angry, because his sons are putting themselves in danger.

Advanced reading skills (pages 63–64)

1 **Look at the writer's description of the sea in the first paragraph. How does she make it seem powerful and menacing?**

'Hurled' is a forceful verb, while the crashing waves are described as 'snuffling', like a hungry animal.

2 **At which point in the text did you know something bad was going to happen? How does the writer hint that it will end in disaster?**

When their father seems anxious and shouts at them to come back it suggests the situation is dangerous. The title of the chapter, 'The Drowning', also suggests that something bad will happen.

CHALLENGE LEVEL 2 UNIT 5

3 Look at the section of the text which begins with 'I was being rushed…' and ends with '…fainter and fainter'. Which of the following statements are true and which are false:

   a) This section is a flashback.

   True

   b) This section is described from the perspective of the main character.

   True

   c) In this section, we learn for certain that Matthew has died.

   False

   d) The writer uses this section to hint, rather than tell us, that something bad has happened.

   True

4 In the same section, how does the writer create a feeling of the main character's confusion?

Sample answers:

- Images of the rescue merge with those of the house and people's faces and voices, all rushing after one another.
- Nothing is explained clearly in the text.
- The main character passes in and out of consciousness.
- Voices are muffled and unclear.
- The meaning of his father's words are not clear.

5 In the final section of the extract (which starts with: 'Master Willim, Master Willim…'), does the story feel as if it is definitely set in a different historical period, or could it be set today? Write a sentence or two explaining your view.

Sample answer:

The section feels as if it is set in a different historical period. Details such as the curtains draped around the bed, the gruel eaten from a wooden bowl and the mention of servants, as well as the nurse calling the narrator 'Master', show that it is unlikely to be set in the modern day.

6 Think about what William and Matthew's father is thinking and feeling. Write down three words to describe the emotions he is experiencing at the end of the opening chapter. Give reasons for your choices. Try to use quotations from the opening chapter, if you can.

Sample answer:

Grief-stricken, exhausted, guilty. The father is feeling grief-stricken, as Matthew has died; he has been 'praying…all day'. It's also clear that the father feels guilty or responsible for Matthew's death, as he cries: 'I tried to save him. I tried, I tried. I could only save one of them.' The father is also exhausted after the dramatic events of the day and the all-night vigil.

Early Bird: Riddle *(page 64)*

> **Can you solve this riddle? 'Give me food, and I will live; give me water, and I will die. What am I?'**
> Fire or thirst

Challenge Level 2: Unit 6

2.6 Pet Care

Basic reading skills (pages 67–68)

Ferrets

1. Read the first paragraph. Based on this paragraph, decide whether each statement is true or false.

   a) Ferrets live underground.

   False

   b) Ferrets can be useful because of their agility in tunnels.

   True

   c) Ferrets were a nuisance at the wedding of Charles and Diana.

   False

   d) Ferrets dig tunnels.

   False

   e) Ferrets enjoy being underground.

   True

   f) Ferrets live for 6–8 years, on average.

   True

2. Pick out three adjectives that the writer uses to describe the positive side of ferrets' behaviour and character.

   Sample answer:

   Comical, loving, playful

3. If you have a ferret in your home, why do you have to be careful where you walk or sit?

   Because they often hide away

4. What is the Latin word that the name 'ferret' derives from?

   Furonem

5. How can you reduce the risk of a ferret developing cancer?

   Have them spayed or neutered at an early age

6. What does the Latin name for 'ferret' mean in English?

   Thief

7. What is the minimum amount of protein required in a ferret's diet?

   32%

8. What colour is an albino ferret?

   White (with pink eyes)

9. Name two foods you should avoid giving ferrets.

   Sample answers – choose two of:
   - Chocolate
   - Liquorice

- Onions
- Nuts

Gerbils

1 According to the text, which of these statements are true or false?

   a) Gerbils never live more than five years.

   False

   b) You should never keep a gerbil on its own but always with others.

   False

   c) The most common gerbil is the Mongolian gerbil.

   True

   d) In the 19th century, gerbils were sent from Europe to China.

   False

   e) Gerbils make great pets.

   True or false (depending on the student's opinion)

2 According to the text, what should you do if your gerbil is sneezing or has matted fur?

   Seek veterinary advice

3 Why do gerbils have fur beneath their paws?

   To protect them from the heat of the desert sand

4 Name two illnesses that gerbils can suffer from, according to the article.

   Sample answers – choose two of:
   - Epilepsy
   - Tyzzer's disease
   - Dental problems
   - Tumours
   - Inner ear problems

5 What should gerbils be fed?

   Gerbil mix with small slices of fresh fruit and vegetables

6 According to the article, how much do gerbils cost?

   £5–£20

7 What three materials can be used for gerbil bedding?

   Sawdust, wood shavings or paper nesting material

8 How should you get a gerbil used to your scent?

   You should hold your hand in the cage and stroke the gerbil gently.

CHALLENGE LEVEL 2 UNIT 6

Advanced reading skills (pages 69–70)

1 Copy the grid below and use it to compare information about ferrets and gerbils found in the article. In each box, add a few key words that best sum up each feature of the animal.

Sample answer:

	FERRET	**GERBIL**
Temperament	Comical, loving, playful	Enjoy human contact, timid
Space requirements	Ferrets like to run free; block holes and tight spaces; use the largest metal cage	Gerbils enjoy wild, underground, tunnel-filled environments.
Advantages	Comical, loving, playful, amusing; expert cable layers; can live with you like a cat	Enjoy human contact
Disadvantages	They often hide away so you need to be careful where you walk or sit; prone to many diseases	Timid; can suffer from epilepsy, Tyzzer's disease, dental problems, tumours and inner ear problems

2 You have been asked to contribute to an 'Ask an Expert' website. Now that you have read about keeping both gerbils and ferrets as pets, how would you respond to this email question?

'Dear Expert, I live in a small house and have my own bedroom. I would like a pet that is fun to own but doesn't take a lot of work. Should I choose a ferret or gerbil? Yours, Asha'

Write down your response, outlining the reasons for your choice.

Sample answer:

You need a ferret. Ferrets are comical, fun-loving creatures which only require as much attention as a pet cat. You just need to be careful about blocking any holes and tight spaces that it may get trapped in.

3 How can you tell that the writer of the article is not taking the subject too seriously? Use quotations from the text to support your answer.

Sample answer:

He begins each section in a jokey way, talking about the Royal Wedding ('if they're good enough for a princess') and hobbits ('why *do* hobbits have furry feet?').

4 Write down three features of the layout of the text that you think help the reader to take in the information quickly. Then suggest one way in which the layout could be improved.

Sample answer:

The article is easy to read because the writer:
- uses a clear, large font
- uses subheadings to break the text up
- includes key information at the start, e.g. life span and cost.

It could be improved by shortening the 'care requirements' section in the ferret article or including more images.

CHALLENGE LEVEL 2 UNIT 6

5 **From the entire article, choose an example of:**

  a) **a statistic**

  Sample answer:

  Ferrets live six to eight years on average.

  b) **a factual statement**

  Sample answer:

  Ferrets are carnivorous.

  c) **a question used to get the reader's interest**

  Sample answer:

  '…why *do* hobbits have furry feet?'

  d) **an opinion**

  Sample answer:

  Gerbils are ideal for Tolkien lovers.

  e) **simple vocabulary**

  Sample answer:

  Gerbils are best kept in groups.

  f) **complex vocabulary.**

  Sample answer:

  Lethargic

Early Bird: Word generator (page 70)

How many words can you create from the letters in 'animals'?

Sample answers:

aim, man, nil, sin, aims, alas, mail, main, sail, slim, slam, alias, mails, nails, nasal, slain, snail, lamina, salami

Challenge Level 3: Unit 1

3.1 Make 'em Win!

Basic reading skills (page 74)

1 **Look at paragraph one. How many people does Clive Woodward introduce to the team?**

   Two

2 **Look at paragraph two. What do we learn from this paragraph about how Clive Woodward is feeling?**

   Proud and privileged to be in the post

3 **Again in paragraph two, in your own words, explain why he decides to pick a team of 30 men.**

   Sample answer:

   He decides that he needs to select a team of 30 men because there are currently too many rugby players to carry out any effective training.

4 **In the fourth paragraph, he writes: 'Even Roger raised his eyebrow at that one'. In your own words, say what 'raised his eyebrow' means here.**

   Sample answer:

   He was surprised or curious.

5 **Look at paragraph five. Clive Woodward says the following about the team: 'we're going to rebuild it all from the ground up'. What does he mean?**

   He means that he is going to make radical changes affecting all areas from bottom to top, creating something entirely new.

6 **Clive Woodward refers to a few of the 'seasoned' players (paragraph five). Which of these words best explains what the adjective 'seasoned' means: 'sunburnt', 'old', 'experienced' or 'angry'?**

   Experienced

7 **Look at the last section of the text. Clive Woodward has asked the players if they have any questions and none of them do.**

   a) **Which of the following statements do you think is definitely not the reason why no one asks a question: 'The players are bored by the speech'; 'The players are stunned by what they have heard'; 'The players can't think of anything to ask'; 'The players just want to start practising'; or 'The players are angry at the way they have been treated'?**

   The players are angry at the way they have been treated.

   b) **Which statement in your opinion is the most likely explanation for why no one speaks?**

   Sample answer:

   It's most likely that they don't speak because they are stunned by the information given in the speech.

CHALLENGE LEVEL 3 UNIT 1

Advanced reading skills (page 75)

1 Look at Clive Woodward's opening sentence: 'Good morning, gentlemen'. Instead of 'gentlemen' he could have addressed them as 'team' or as 'lads', etc. Why do you think he uses 'gentlemen'?

Sample answer:

He is treating them with respect and making a formal and important statement to them.

2 a) Which of the following words best describes the way Clive Woodward speaks to the players: 'tough', 'aggressive', 'funny', 'motivational' or 'direct'?

Direct

b) Write down one phrase or sentence from the text which supports your choice.

Sample answers:

- 'I am going to pick a squad of 30 from you'
- 'I will select you on your merit'
- 'please listen carefully'
- 'If you're here for any other reason, you're in the wrong room'
- 'That all stops now.'
- 'It won't be easy.'
- 'The message for you all is simple.'

4 How can you tell that this text is a speech rather than an essay or letter?

Sample answers:

- He makes it clear that he is addressing a room full of people.
- He includes people's reactions to his words.
- He includes inverted commas, showing that he is speaking.

5 In his speech, Clive Woodward uses the pronouns 'I', 'me' and 'you' a lot. Explain why you think this is.

Sample answer:

He is building a relationship between himself and individuals, making the content of the speech personal, showing what he wants as a manager and making the impact more direct.

Early Bird: Riddle (page 75)

> **Can you solve this riddle? 'What goes around the world but stays in a corner?'**
> Postage stamp

Challenge Level 3: Unit 2

3.2 Attack of the Killer Bees!

Basic reading skills (page 78)

1 **What was the first sign that there would be a bee attack?**
 The sound of the bees

2 **What caused the bees to attack?**
 The group had disturbed the bees' colony.

3 **Where was the writer's friend John when the bee attack began?**
 He was on the rock face ahead of the writer, close to the water.

4 **Why had the friends gone to the river in the first place?**
 To cool off

5 **What type of bees were they?**
 Giant honey bees

6 **How long do the friends have to remain in the water?**
 Three hours

7 **John was 'lethally allergic to stings'. In your own words, explain what this means.**
 It means that he has such a strong reaction to stings that he could die if stung.

8 **Name one other bad experience with animals the writer says she has had.**
 Sample answers:
 - She was attacked by wild dogs.
 - She was nearly trampled to death by an elephant.

Advanced reading skills (page 79)

1 **Look at the writer's first sentence. She could have written 'I was 18 and backpacking around India with friends'; instead, she starts paragraph two with that sentence. What effect does her opening sentence have on the reader and why?**
 It starts with the action – the bee attack – which grabs the reader's interest immediately.

2 **The writer says she is with a group of friends.**
 a) **How many do you think there were and how can you tell?**
 There were four of them in the group, including the writer; she says this in paragraph two: '...four of us decided to cool off'.
 b) **How many do you learn the name of?**
 One: John

CHALLENGE LEVEL 3 UNIT 2

3 In order to describe to the reader what the bee attack was like, the writer uses words relating to different senses. Write down one word she uses for each of these senses:

a) sound

Sample answers:

Heard, hum, louder, noise, loud

b) sight

Sample answers:

Saw, smoke, cloud, swarmed, swelled, melon, red

c) touch.

Sample answers:

Sting, pain, agony, bumps

4 In her final sentence the writer says: 'I'll always be thankful that the bees attacked me and not my friends'. However, at least one of her friends is also stung. What does she mean?

She was the main target of their attack; this was less dangerous than the bees attacking John (and maybe the other two) as she was immune to their poison.

Early Bird: Anagrams (page 80)

> **Rearrange the letters in these anagrams to spell out the names of three capital cities.**
>
> 1 more: Rome
>
> 2 smart dame: Amsterdam
>
> 3 my toxic ice: Mexico City

Challenge Level 3: Unit 3

3.3 Quacking Ducks and Icebergs!

Basic reading skills (page 84)

1 **Where did the writer think that he had heard the echo of a duck's quack before?**

   He thinks he has heard duck quack echoes around duck ponds.

2 **What makes the author think that lots of people believe that duck quacks do not echo?**

   Information on the Internet implies this.

3 **In your own words, say what the writer means when he suggests that ponds surrounded by trees and bushes are 'not exactly prime echo-generating conditions'.**

   The writer means that echoes are less likely to be generated where the environment is soft and absorbent.

4 **Does the writer agree or disagree that duck quacks do not have an echo?**

   He disagrees.

5 **Why is Antarctica's sheet-ice so important?**

   It contains around 70% of the world's fresh water.

6 **What word could the writer have used instead of 'barmy'?**

   Sample answers:

   Foolish, silly, mad, irrational, fanciful, stupid, bonkers, daft, ridiculous

7 **Why would an iceberg not completely melt if dragged from Antarctica?**

   It takes an enormous amount of heat to melt an iceberg.

8 **What word could the writer have used instead of 'lug'?**

   Sample answers:

   Draw, pull, haul, drag, tug, tow

9 **Which of the following reasons is the main one that the writer gives for the iceberg idea not being practical: 'Icebergs melt'; 'It is too expensive'; 'It is too hot'; 'It is too complicated'; or 'Places needing water are too far inland'?**

   It is too expensive.

Advanced reading skills (pages 84–85)

1 **The writer uses a mixture of scientific language and informal expression. Write down one word or phrase which is technical; write down one word or phrase which is very informal.**

   Sample answers:

   - Technical: sound-absorbent; echo-generating conditions; staccato pattern
   - Informal: baffled; quick trawl; enough already; barmy; lug

CHALLENGE LEVEL 3 UNIT 3

2 **Summarize, in two sentences, the answers to the questions about duck quacks and icebergs.**

Sample answer:

Duck quacks do have echoes, but it is hard to hear them because ducks live surrounded by soft vegetation, which absorbs the sound, and the repetitive noise of the quack masks any echoes. Icebergs could be towed from Antarctica without melting substantially, but the cost of doing this and distributing the water to drought-stricken areas is too expensive.

3 **Look at the iceberg text. Draw a sketch with labels to show the problems that would be involved in trying to drag an iceberg from the Antarctic to a place in need of fresh water.**

Students should have drawn a sketch of an iceberg being dragged by a ship from a land mass (Antarctica). Included should be an arrow indicating passage to a drought-stricken area, e.g. Africa, a power station on the African coast, and pipes running inland. Labels on the sketch may include: 'Antarctica', '100 million ton iceberg', 'powerful ship', 'very strong cable', 'Africa', 'thousands of miles to drought-stricken area' and 'large power station to melt the iceberg'.

4 **The writer combines facts and opinions in both texts. For each text, write down one fact he gives and one opinion.**

Sample answer:

- Ducks – fact: 'Ducks traditionally spend their time on flat ponds...'
- Ducks – opinion: 'I feel sure I have heard the echo of quacks from the underside of bridges and the like.'
- Icebergs – fact: 'The Antarctic ice-sheet contains around 70% of the world's fresh water...'
- Icebergs – opinion: 'For the time being, berg-towing remains an engineer's pipe-dream.'

Early Bird: Word ladder (page 85)

> **Changing just one letter at a time, get from the word TAME to the word WILD in four steps.**
>
> TAME, TIME, TILE, WILE, WILD

Challenge Level 3: Unit 4

3.4 Work Experience? No, Thanks!

Basic reading skills (pages 89–90)

1 From the article, would you say that the following statements are true or false?

   a) The writer states that he hated work experience as a student.

   False

   b) The writer believes that work experience is a waste of time.

   True

   c) The writer says that work experience costs schools a lot of money.

   False

   d) The writer says that a small number of students benefit from work experience.

   True

2 Write down one reason the writer gives to support his view that work experience is a bad idea.

   Sample answers:

   • It's a lot of work for little effect.
   • The experience is demeaning and menial.
   • There are more important things to do at school.
   • It doesn't inspire children to find a career path.
   • School shouldn't be about preparing children for work.
   • It is too soon to expose children to the world of work.
   • The students are an inconvenience in the placements.

3 The writer says: 'Of course there are kids who are transformed by the experience'. Write down one example he gives of the benefits of work experience.

   Sample answers:

   • 'It can bring lessons and ambitions into a sharp focus.'
   • 'Those following a vocational pathway may indeed find out things that will help them.'

4 The writer says that children 'should be allowed to be children'. Which one of the following does he not mean: 'Children do not need to learn about the world of work until they are older'; 'Children should not be encouraged to grow up too early'; 'Children are too stupid to work' or 'Children can experience work at the right time in their development'?

   Children are too stupid to work.

5 Write down, in your own words, what the writer means when he says: 'we send out the inadequate into an incomplete version of the world of work'.

Sample answer:

The writer means that because young people do not really have the skills, they do not gain experience of real working practices on their placements. Also, students can only partially understand the 'world of work' on a short placement where they are completing menial tasks.

Advanced reading skills (pages 90–91)

2 Look at the first paragraph of the article. The writer could have left out sentence two ('Yes, you have guessed it'). Explain why you think he includes it.

Sample answer:

It directly addresses the reader, grabbing their attention; it also gets the reader on the writer's side by assuming they hold the same opinion.

3 Choose one sentence from the article which you think best sums up the writer's attitude to work experience. Write it down and then explain why you have chosen it.

Sample answer:

'For many of our children it is a complete waste of time.' The writer provides many reasons why work experience is a complete waste of time for many young people, but he does also suggest (briefly) that some students benefit.

Early Bird: Anagrams (page 91)

> **Rearrange the letters in these anagrams to spell out the names of three *Harry Potter* characters.**
>
> 1 let mob not live long: Neville Longbottom
> 2 slyly rude dude: Dudley Dursley
> 3 I sure had grub: Rubeus Hagrid

Challenge Level 3: Unit 5

3.5 Heading to a New School

Basic reading skills (page 95)

1. **In paragraph one, why is Sam Arthur Tack close to tears?**

   He is going to boarding school, and is nervous and sad about leaving his parents behind.

2. **Why is the train running late?**

   There is a mix up over staff in the buffet car.

3. **What are the school colours?**

   Black and gold

4. **What is the name of the other boy from Ribblestrop school?**

   Jacob Ruskin

5. **The writer says: 'the boy yanked open the door'. Write down what 'yanked' means.**

   Pulled suddenly

6. **Why is Sam feeling faint?**

   He hadn't eaten breakfast and he is nervous about leaving home and starting at a new school.

7. **Once they are on the train, the other Ribblestrop student says: 'You blub if you want to'. Write down what 'blub' means.**

   Cry

Advanced reading skills (page 96)

1. **The author describes Sam's voice as 'a cracked whisper'. In your own words, say what you think this means.**

   Sample answer:

   It was very quiet and unsteady because he was so emotional.

2. **How do Sam's mother and father react differently to his going away to school?**

   His mother is emotional, but his father is straightforward and positive.

3. **Sam's parents use some words which show that they belong to a different era. Write down two examples of their old-fashioned vocabulary.**

   Sample answer:

   Blast it, blasted

4. **Which of the following words do you think best describes Ruskin: 'welcoming', 'aggressive', 'clumsy', 'impolite' or 'enthusiastic'? Write a sentence explaining your choice of word.**

   Sample answer:

   Enthusiastic. Jacob Ruskin is a very enthusiastic character, as he expresses a passion for Ribblestrop school and is keen to take Sam under his wing.

5 **The writer describes the arrival of the elderly woman into the carriage. How does he make us feel that she is not very nice?**

Sample answers:

- She has a grating voice.
- She is severe looking.
- She smells bad.
- She is careless in the way she pushes her luggage.
- She rudely refuses help.
- She 'barks' into her phone.

6 What hints does the writer give that Ribblestrop will not be an ordinary school?

Sample answers:

- The school blazer has vivid stripes.
- The school won't mind if Sam's cap is lost.
- Some students leave because they can't stand it, but others love it.
- Dr Norcross-Webb has a strange name.

Early Bird: Anagrams (page 96)

> **Rearrange the letters in these anagrams to spell out the names of three school subjects.**
>
> **1** shy riot: history
> **2** hammiest cat: mathematics
> **3** my richest: chemistry

Challenge Level 4: Unit 1

4.1 I Fell 6000 Feet and Survived!

Basic reading skills (pages 99–100)

1 **True or false: James Boole was flying over Russia to do a skydive?**
   True

2 **Look at paragraph two. What is the 'Kamchatka'? Is it: a volcano, high mountains, an area of ice or a region of volcanoes and ice?**
   A region of volcanoes and ice

3 **How long has James Boole been involved in skydiving?**
   12 years

4 **What is the first sign that something has gone wrong with the skydive?**
   The writer could see the texture of the snow and ice, which meant he was too close to the ground and should have opened his parachute earlier.

5 **After the crash landing, the writer feels both 'elation' (extreme joy) and 'fear'. What causes each emotion?**
   He feels elation because he is still alive; he feels fear because he knows he has broken his back.

6 **Look at the final paragraph. In your own words, explain why James Boole feels conflicted about whether to continue to skydive.**
   Sample answer:
   He wants a balance between his hobby and spending time with his family, and he knows that the hobby could cost him his life.

7 **How deep was the crater that James Boole left in the snow after his accident?**
   1 metre deep

8 **Approximately how many jumps has James Boole completed during his involvement in skydiving?**
   Around 2500 jumps

9 **At what distance had James Boole intended to open his parachute?**
   From 150 to 200 metres

Advanced reading skills (page 100)

1 **Which of these words do you think best describes James Boole: 'reckless', 'big-headed', 'calm', 'brave' or 'worried'? Write a sentence explaining your choice and provide a detail or quotation from the text to support it.**
   Sample answer:
   James is brave because he is going to do another jump even though he nearly died. He says: 'I'll definitely do one more, then see how I feel.'

CHALLENGE LEVEL 4 UNIT 1

2 When he realizes his parachute has not opened, James Boole writes: 'Terror gripped my heart and stomach, the darkest of darkness'. Which of the following statements does not accurately explain his choice of words: 'He chooses language that is poetic'; 'He chooses language that makes his emotions more vivid'; 'He chooses language that makes it feel as if he is about to die' or 'He chooses language that makes his feelings more dramatic'?

   He chooses language that is poetic.

3 In paragraph five, the writer says he was 'overwhelmed by sadness'. Think of another word which means 'overwhelmed'.

   Sample answers:

   Overcome, overpowered, engulfed

4 What do you think the writer meant when he states: 'This is going to hurt a lot... or not at all'?

   James Boole was suggesting that he was aware that the fall would either prove fatal (and therefore not hurt at all) or very damaging.

5 James Boole's account uses a number of powerful, vivid descriptions of his experience. Choose one phrase or sentence; write it down and explain why you think it works so well.

   Sample answer:

   'The ground hit me full in the back with the force of a truck' is powerful because from the point of view of the writer it must have seemed that the ground was crashing into him (rather than the other way round), and the comparison with a truck describes its brutal force and directness.

6 Look at the final paragraph. The writer refers to 'Icarus's dream'. See the 'Build your word power' section of this unit to understand the reference. Explain what you think James Boole means when he compares skydiving to this Greek myth.

   Sample answer:

   Skydiving must feel like the closest thing to actually flying, but the writer is also hinting at the part of the myth where Icarus flies too close to the sun and his recklessness results in a catastrophic fall.

Early Bird: Word generator (page 101)

> **How many words can you create from the letters in 'adventurous'?**
>
> *Sample answers:*
>
> dot, eat, end, era, nod, not, oat, one, ran, rod, rat, sat, set, sun, tar, ten, vat, van, ants, aunt, dart, dear, dent, done, dots, near, node, nuts, oats, rota, runs, sand, send, sent, sore, star, sure, tend, toad, tore, user, vase, vast, vote, arose, arson, dares, dates, donut, earns, nurse, ovens, reads, roads, saved, saver, snout, snore, tears, tread, tuned, voted, arouse, donate, duvets, ornate, outrun, reason, snared, soared, stared, tavern, trends, unsure, untrue, arduous, devours, roasted, rodents, snorted, treason, ravenous, unsorted

Challenge Level 4: Unit 2

4.2 The Meat We Eat

Basic reading skills (page 106)

Text A: Newspaper article

1 **What creates the artificial darkness?**

   Dim blue lights

2 **What is a CAS?**

   Controlled atmosphere stunning – a way of making the birds unconscious

3 **How long does it take for the turkeys to become unconscious?**

   Up to 10 seconds

4 **How long does it take for the turkeys to die?**

   Approximately two minutes

Text B: 'Song of the Battery Hen' by Edwin Brock

1 **Look at the first section of the poem. Using the writer's description, draw a brief sketch of the accommodation, using arrows and words to label its main features.**

   Ensure that the sketch includes reference to these features: concrete floor, four white walls, sheet-iron roof, fan, fluorescent lighting.

2 **Write down one phrase which tells us what the hen telling her story looks like.**

   Sample answers:

   Orange-red comb; yellow beak; auburn feathers

Advanced reading skills (page 106)

Text A: Newspaper article

2 **What do you think the writer means when she describes 'Wallace-and-Gromit style "rubber fingers"'?**

   She is referring to the automatic way in which the fingers move in the machinery, a bit like animation. She is also suggesting that the fingers look like a wacky invention from a fictional programme or film.

3 **Do you agree or disagree with the following statement: 'The writer describes the turkey farm in a neutral way which does not reveal her own opinion'? Say whether you think the statement is true, partly true or untrue. Explain your reasoning, using quotations from the text.**

   Sample answer:

   The statement is true, because straightforward descriptive language is used rather than emotive language, for example, 'freshly killed', 'their necks are cut by hand' and 'final trussing or butchery'. There are very few adjectives and even these are used in a balanced way, for example their 'short' lives are balanced by their 'swift and painless' end.

CHALLENGE LEVEL 4 UNIT 2

Text B: 'Song of the Battery Hen' by Edwin Brock

1 **Look at the first sentence of the poem. Do you think this is supposed to be sarcastic (saying one thing but meaning the opposite) or genuine? Explain your answer.**

Sample answer:

The hen is being genuine, as she seems to appreciate the material conditions, but the writer is being sarcastic, as his view is that the hens are cruelly crammed together in the accommodation.

2 **The hen who narrates the poem seems proud to be an individual, telling us about the colours of her feathers and the sound she makes. How does the writer show that she is not as individual as she believes?**

Sample answer:

The precise directions for locating her show how she is one of a large number of hens all penned together in rows.

3 **Twice in section three of the poem, the hen says: 'Listen'. What do you think the writer is suggesting about her or her environment?**

Sample answer:

The poet is suggesting that the hen thinks she has an individual voice and she wants to be heard. He also implies that she longs to belong to the outside world – she wants us to 'Listen' to the cockerel.

4 **In section three, the hen describes the cockerel at the broiler house. What does this reveal about her?**

Sample answer:

It implies that she is sad to be separated from the cockerel, who represents the free life she dreams of.

5 **Look at the last line of the poem. Comment on the use of the word 'blessed'.**

Sample answer:

Blessed is a religious word, which continues the reference to God in the previous line. In one sense the hen is blessed, as she appreciates the accommodation; in another sense the writer is being sarcastic.

Early Bird: Anagrams (page 107)

> **Rearrange the letters in these anagrams to spell out the names of three Shakespeare plays.**
>
> 1 a module jointer: Romeo and Juliet
> 2 like gran: King Lear
> 3 sue jails a cur: Julius Caesar

Challenge Level 4: Unit 3

4.3 Putting the Boot into Skiing

Basic reading skills (page 112)

1 **Look at the first two paragraphs. Name three skiing hazards that Jeremy Clarkson writes about.**

   Sample answer:

   Hypothermia, risk of severe injury and very expensive clothing

2 **According to the writer, what is the main difference between skiing and snowboarding?**

   When snowboarding, you have no control over your direction.

3 **Copy and complete the grid below. Decide whether the statements are definitely true, probably true, definitely false or probably false, depending on what the writer included in his article. Mark your choice with a tick.**

   Sample answer:

	DEFINITELY TRUE	PROBABLY TRUE	DEFINITELY FALSE	PROBABLY FALSE
Jeremy Clarkson enjoys skiing.	✓			
He thinks he is a good skier.				✓
He thinks skiing is dangerous.		✓		
He likes some of the food served on ski holidays.				✓
He thinks the clothing is expensive.	✓			

4 **In the penultimate paragraph, the writer says 'you will come home after a week with a face like a barn owl'. Say in your own words what you think he means.**

   Sample answer:

   Your eyes will look unnaturally large because of the effect of wearing goggles in the strong sunlight (i.e. odd tan lines).

5 **Is Jeremy Clarkson totally against skiing? Summarize his views about the activity in one sentence.**

   Sample answer:

   He mostly thinks that skiing is uncomfortable, expensive and dangerous, but admits that it can, briefly, be fabulous.

Advanced reading skills (page 112)

1 **Look at the first paragraph of the article. Write down two literary techniques that Jeremy Clarkson uses to grab his readers' attention.**

   Sample answers:

   - Direct address, using the second person
   - Rhetorical questions

CHALLENGE LEVEL 4 UNIT 3

- Use of humour
- Delaying making the subject matter (skiing) clear until the final sentence of the first paragraph

2 Find and write down two examples each of:

a) exaggeration

Sample answers:

All your money; stand in a fridge; better than evens chance of a serious accident; ski pole sticking out of his eye; left foot on back to front; thigh muscles catch fire; travelling at 700 mph; five newly formed paraplegics every day

b) sarcasm

Sample answers:

'For your next holiday, why don't you take all your money and put it on the fire?'; 'The food at ski resorts is cooked by people whose only qualification for the job is that they are called Arabella.'

c) informal language

Sample answers:

Better than evens chance; a chap; I'm rubbish; 'fraid not; the thing is

d) enthusiasm.

Sample answers:

Whizzing along; perfect blue dome; happy, giggling children; deserted, freshly pisted slope; view that is unparalleled; no feeling quite like it; perfect happiness

3 **Columnists, like Jeremy Clarkson, often try to deliberately annoy their readers. Think of three people or groups who might be offended or upset by what he has written.**

Sample answers:

Ski holiday organizers; chefs at ski resorts; Russians

4 **One of the ways Jeremy Clarkson tries to make us laugh is through his use of stereotypes. Choose two from the list below and, in your own words, explain what he is saying about: snow-boarders, people called Arabella, and readers of the** *Guardian*.

Sample answers:

- He describes snow-boarders as baggy-trousered teenagers with no control over their direction.
- He describes ski resort cooks as young women with no experience or skills.
- He describes *Guardian* readers as only interested in museums.

Early Bird: Anagrams (page 113)

Rearrange the letters in these anagrams to spell out the names of three countries.

1 mafia tease destruction: United States of America
2 sooty vicar: Ivory Coast
3 big mule: Belgium

Challenge Level 4: Unit 4

4.4 My Pet Human

Basic reading skills (page 117)

1 **Cat describes himself as 'a well-balanced cat'. Think of another word which means 'well-balanced'.**

   Sample answer:

   Versatile

2 **Cat says: 'I like her no-nonsense attitude to life'. What does he mean by 'no-nonsense'?**

   Sample answer:

   He means straight and direct.

3 **Write down two details which show that Cat thinks he is in charge.**

   Sample answers:

   He says that: he owns the male; that the male can't think; that he changed the male's name; that he calls the male to feed him; that he's given the male a 'flap' (door).

4 **What is it about the elastic band that makes it seem 'pathetic' and 'so limited' to Cat?**

   Cat thinks that the elastic band is pathetic because it always does the same thing: 'stretch, stretch, ping'.

5 **Why does Cat decide to give his pet human a fancy name?**

   Cat gives his pet human a fancy name because he thinks that 'Man' is too ugly. He claims that he gave the human a name he can be proud of.

6 **Cat argues that risks have to be taken with the human because 'it's the price of being free'. In your own words, explain what he means.**

   Sample answer:

   The disadvantage of allowing the human freedom is that he runs the risk of being harmed outside the house.

Advanced reading skills (page 117)

1 **Which of the following words do you think best sums up Cat's attitude: 'mad', 'strange', 'confused', 'misguided' or 'arrogant'? Write down your choice and then, in a sentence, explain why you think it is the most appropriate.**

   Sample answer:

   Cat is misguided, because he thinks he is in charge whereas he is really the man's pet.

CHALLENGE LEVEL 4 UNIT 4

3 Why is the line 'I never miaow down to him' funny?

Sample answer:

It is funny because it is a cat version of 'I never speak down to him'.

Early Bird: Word generator (page 118)

How many words can you create from the letters in 'human being'?

Sample answers:

bug, ham, man, amen, bean, huge, hung, main, begun, binge, image, neigh, enigma, guinea, gunman, humane, hangmen, inhuman, numbing, unhinge

Challenge Level 5: Unit 1

5.1 Genius or Mad Man?

Basic reading skills (page 122)

1 In the first paragraph, the writer names two swimming aids that are currently used. What are they?

Flippers and snorkels

2 Are the following statements true or false?

a) Mr Pedrazzolli is from Italy.

True

b) He married an Italian woman.

False

c) He set up business as a wholesale and export looking-glass manufacturer.

True

d) His idea was to help people to swim faster.

True

3 What do the swimming umbrellas look like and how do they work? Using all of the information in the text, draw a picture of what you understand them to be like. Use labels to explain their features.

Students should draw an image which includes the following features: a small umbrella-shaped instrument, which is hand-held, and which clearly closes up when the hands/arms move forwards and opens out when the hands/arms move backwards.

4 The writer of the article tests out some swimming umbrellas. Name one positive feature of the invention and two problems that the writer identifies.

Sample answer:

They provided a good grip on the water, but they were slow to open and too heavy.

5 Why does the writer finally give up on using them?

He decided he could swim better without them.

Advanced reading skills (page 122)

1 The writer calls the inventor 'Mr Pedrazzolli'. What effect does not using the inventor's first name have?

Sample answer:

It is formal and old-fashioned, so it helps to place the subject matter in the past. Also, it makes it seem like the writer respects the inventor.

2 Look at the first sentence. The writer uses the verb 'flash'. Is this a good choice of vocabulary? In a sentence, explain your answer.

Sample answer:

It is a good choice because it suggests the fast movement in a visual way, like a flash of lightning. It is also almost onomatopoeic.

CHALLENGE LEVEL 5 UNIT 1

3 In the second sentence of the text, the writer uses the adjective 'splendid'. Write down another word with a similar meaning that he might have used instead.

Sample answers:

Outstanding, spectacular, brilliant, eye-catching

4 Read this comment on the text and decide whether you agree or disagree with it: 'You can tell from the article that the writer admires and respects Mr Pedrazzolli'.

a) Find two points from the text that support this view.

Sample answers:

- He calls him Mr Pedrazzolli, which is a formal mode of address.
- He describes the umbrellas as a 'splendid' invention.
- He suggests that Mr Pedrazzolli thought hard about his invention.
- He admits that the umbrellas gave a good grip on the water.
- He takes time to try the invention out by making it.

b) Is there anything in the text that suggests it is not true?

Sample answers:

- By trying the invention out, and describing the results in such detail, he seems to take the inventor almost too seriously when the idea is so comical.
- He lists several defects of the invention in the final paragraph.
- He repeats 'hitherto impossible' which may be poking fun.

5 If you were the editor of this article, what advice would you give the writer about how to make the story of Mr Pedrazzolli's inventions more interesting to younger readers? Think about how you might present the text (the layout) and how the invention could be described.

Sample answer:

Use: shorter paragraphs, subheadings, a more interesting font, larger point size and more colour. Do not quote from the original patent, as the language is too difficult. Use shorter sentences with simpler vocabulary. Use striking descriptive language to help readers picture what the swimmer does and the effects of using the invention (both intended and actual).

Early Bird: Word ladder (page 123)

> **Changing just one letter at a time, get from the word READ to the word BOOK in five steps.**
>
> READ, ROAD, ROOD, ROOK, BOOK

Challenge Level 5: Unit 2

5.2 Badger Watch

Basic reading skills (page 127)

1 **Look again at the first paragraph. Name two essential conditions for badger-watching at night.**

   A warm evening with little wind

2 **During their night-time outing, name three different creatures that the family see.**

   Sample answers:

   Badgers, rabbits, sheep, blackbirds

3 **Why is it important to be downwind of the badgers?**

   It is important so that the wind will not bring the human scent to the badgers' sensitive noses.

4 **At the end of the extract, the writer says: 'We were of the mountain'. Which of these do you think gives the best description of what he means: 'They are covered in soil'; 'They feel they belong to nature'; 'They are overjoyed to see the badgers'; or 'They feel part of the badger family'? Give reasons for your answer.**

   Sample answer:

   They feel they belong to nature: 'of the mountain' suggests they were almost made of the same material as the mountain.

5 **Look at the last word of the extract. Think of another word with a similar meaning to 'bewitching'.**

   Sample answers:

   Spellbinding, magical, transporting, enthralling, enchanting

Advanced reading skills (page 127)

1 **Look at the opening sentence when the writer describes the 'first hot yawns of summer'. What do you think he means by the word 'yawns'?**

   Sample answer:

   The days are hot and long, which makes you sleepy. The days themselves are described as sleepy, for effect.

2 **The writer uses the verb 'chorused'. What image does this verb create in your mind?**

   The boys speak excitedly and at the same time, like a chorus singing.

3 **Which of these descriptions best summarizes the way the writer feels during the badger-watching: 'Bored at first; interested later'; 'Excited at first; inspired later'; 'Nervous at first; speechless later'; or 'Worried at first; amazed later'? Write a sentence explaining your choice.**

   Sample answer:

   Excited at first; inspired later. 'Excited' is suggested by such phrases as 'fixed our eyes' and 'barely breathed'. Afterwards words such as 'magical', 'amazing', 'epiphany', 'reverently' and 'blessed' suggest they are inspired.

4 **The writer describes the blackbirds as 'pink-pinking in the hedges'. In your own words, say what you think the writer means.**

Sample answer:

The words are used to describe the repeated 'pink-pink' sound of the blackbirds. The description is onomatopoeic.

5 **The writer uses a number of similes to capture what he sees. Similes help to make a picture more vivid by comparing one thing with another, using the words 'like' or 'as'. Copy the grid below and, for each example, explain what image is created in your mind. The last example of a simile has been left blank; you will have to find your own example from the text.**

Sample answer:

SIMILE	IMAGE
'Vermilion berries, like clusters of balloons'	Shiny red balls grouped together in bunches
'Jenny ducking their greetings like a film star trying to go incognito'	Keeping her head down and moving fast
'We felt the dusk's harmony like concert-goers'	Eagerly and actively listening to the sounds of the evening and taking in the colours and images around them
'We became as still as stumps'	Sitting motionless and squat

6 **In a short paragraph, explain how the writer uses language to convey a vivid sense of what it was like to be in the woods that night.**

Sample answer:

He uses highly descriptive adjectives, such as '<u>curly</u> whispering' and '<u>ringing</u> accusations'; similes such as 'brash and outraged as a burglar alarm'; words engaging the senses, such as 'loud chiming cries', 'nocturne blues' and 'dew smell'; imagery such as 'hot yawns of full summer', 'conjuring himself' and 'senses stretched'; interesting and descriptive verbs such as 'snuffling' and 'beetling'; and a suggestion of deeper meaning with words such as 'epiphany' and 'bewitching'.

Early Bird: Anagrams (page 128)

Rearrange the letters in these anagrams to spell out the names of three different types of animal.

1 emanate: manatee

2 figfare: giraffe

3 the plane: elephant

Challenge Level 5: Unit 3

5.3 The Day the Earth Shook

Basic reading skills (page 132)

1 **How old is the girl?**

Five years old

2 **Draw a sketch of what the scene looks like. Use labels and arrows to highlight any specific details.**

Students should draw a sketch which includes all or most of the following: a rocky beach at bend in river; a steep bank on opposite side; a river that widens downstream; a hide-covered lean-to in the background.

3 **The girl is described as swimming with 'sure strokes'. What does 'sure' mean in this context? Think of another word that the author could have used to convey a similar meaning.**

Sample answers:

Certain, strong, confident

4 **The extract starts off by describing a normal day for the girl. What is the first sign that something unexpected is happening?**

The stone rolling down from the pyramid of pebbles as the earth trembled

5 **Find a phrase or sentence in the text which tells you that the girl's first reaction is surprise, rather than fear.**

Sample answers:

- 'The child looked with surprise'
- 'stared in wonder'

6 **The writer describes 'the foul-breathed gaping maw'. Which of the following statements do not explain the phrase: 'The earth has come alive'; 'A huge creature has surfaced from the earth'; 'The earth is compared to a creature'; 'The earth seems to be attacking the girl'; or 'The earth is falling into a giant hole'?**

'A huge creature has surfaced from the earth', because the phrase describes the earth itself rather than something emerging from it.

7 **In one sentence, using no more than 25 words, describe what actually happens in this extract.**

Sample answer:

A girl in prehistoric times is swimming when there is an earthquake, which destroys her home and leaves her alone and scared.

Advanced reading skills (page 132)

1 **As you read the text, when did you think it was set: in the past, present or future? Are there any actual clues about the time period?**

Sample answer:

The text is set in the past. The only clue to suggest this is the reference to her home as a 'hide covered lean-to'.

CHALLENGE LEVEL 5 UNIT 3

2 Use a spider diagram to show what we learn from the extract about the character of the girl.

Sample answer:

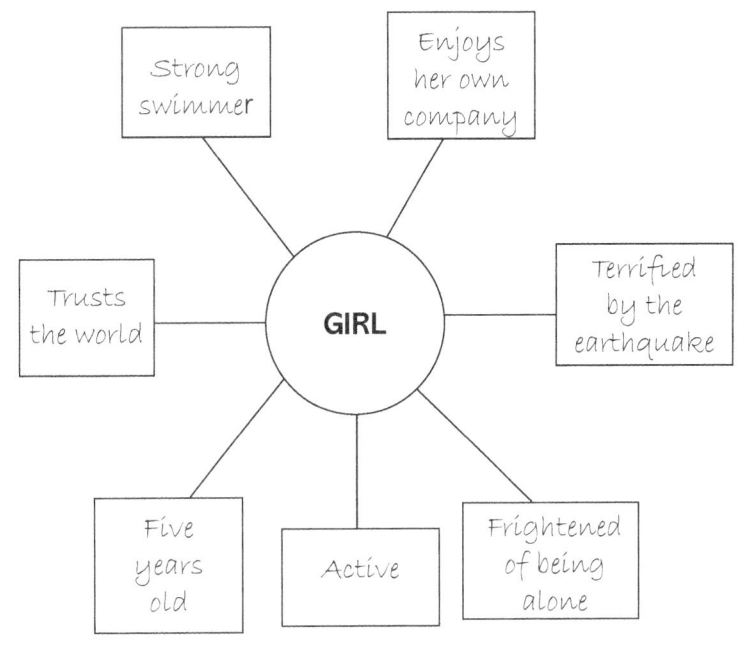

Spider diagram with **GIRL** at the centre, connected to:
- Strong swimmer
- Enjoys her own company
- Terrified by the earthquake
- Frightened of being alone
- Active
- Five years old
- Trusts the world

3 Look again at the first paragraph. Notice the way the author holds back details, not telling us the name of the girl, the place or the other people. Explain what effect this has on the reader.

Sample answer:

It makes the action very immediate and direct, uncluttered by background detail.

4 The writer uses a technique known as personification – making the earth seem as if it has a life of its own, like a creature.

   a) Find an example of personification in the text.

   Sample answers:
   - 'foul-breathed gaping maw'
   - 'earth rose up and threw her down'
   - 'the earth was digesting a meal'

   b) Explain what effect personification has in this part of the story.

   Sample answer:

   It makes the earthquake seem more monstrous and as if it is deliberately trying to be destructive.

Early Bird: Riddle (page 133)

> Can you solve this riddle? 'The beginning of eternity, the end of time and space, the beginning of every end and the end of every place. What am I?'
>
> The letter 'e'

Challenge Level 5: Unit 4

5.4 Iceberg!

Basic reading skills (page 140)

Text A: 'The Titanic Ship: An Invincible Tragedy'

1 In which year did the Titanic set sail?

 1912

2 At which port did the first passengers board the ship?

 Southampton

3 What happened to the small nearby ship, the New York?

 It was sucked into the Titanic's wake; the two ships nearly collided.

4 Which port in Ireland did the Titanic stop at before heading towards New York?

 Queenstown

5 How many lifeboats did the Titanic have?

 20

Text B: *Every Man for Himself* by Beryl Bainbridge

1 The extract contains many names of people who were on board the Titanic. Write down three of them.

 Sample answers – choose three of:

 Hopper, Ginsberg, Rosenfelder, Scurra, McKinlay, Seefax, Mr Andrews

2 In the second sentence, the writer mentions 'life-preservers'. What would we call them today?

 Life jackets

3 One man says that he thinks it is all 'an elaborate hoax'. We do not know his name, but what is he wearing?

 A golfing jacket on top of pyjamas

4 Write down three details which show the text is set in the past. You might choose words people use or details about their clothing.

 Sample answers:

 Life-preservers, wrappers, wireless, stateroom, stockings, steerage class, good chap, top hat

5 Write down one fact we learn from Text A that is not included in Text B; then write down one fact from Text B that is not in Text A.

 Sample answer:

 - 1,523 people drowned (Text A).
 - The mail sacks were stained with damp (Text B).

Advanced reading skills (page 140)

1 Text A comes from a website. Write down three clues that tell you this.

 Sample answer:

 - The text uses short paragraphs.
 - The text is divided into sections.
 - Images are included.

CHALLENGE LEVEL 5 UNIT 4

2 **Text B is from a novel. Write down three clues that tell you this.**

   Sample answers – choose three of:
   - The text tells a story (narrative).
   - It has several named characters.
   - Speech is included.
   - The past tense is used.
   - It includes lots of descriptive detail.
   - The text is told from the point of view of one of the characters.

3 **Text B is told to us through the eyes of a narrator. We do not learn his name in the extract. What else do we learn about him? Use a spider diagram to record any clues about his appearance and personality from the extract.**

   Sample answer:

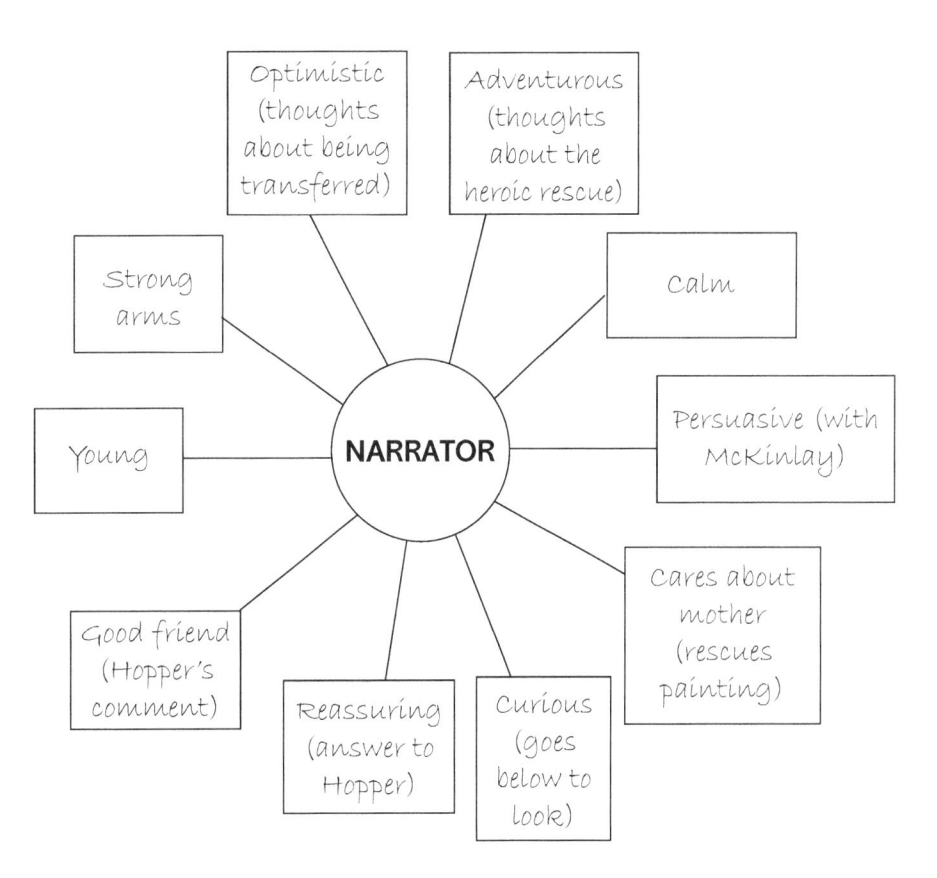

   Spider diagram with NARRATOR in the centre, connected to:
   - Optimistic (thoughts about being transferred)
   - Adventurous (thoughts about the heroic rescue)
   - Strong arms
   - Calm
   - Young
   - Persuasive (with McKinlay)
   - Good friend (Hopper's comment)
   - Cares about mother (rescues painting)
   - Reassuring (answer to Hopper)
   - Curious (goes below to look)

5 **Compare the two texts by reading the statements below. For each one decide whether the statement applies to Text A, Text B, both texts or neither text.**

   a) The text contains no facts.

   Neither text. While Text B is not a factual account, it does contain a few facts.

   b) The text contains no opinions.

   Neither text

   c) The text uses high-level language.

   Both texts

CHALLENGE LEVEL 5 UNIT 4

   d) **The text is easy to follow.**
   Both texts

   e) **The text helps me to understand what happened on board the Titanic.**
   Both texts

   f) **The text provides useful details about the context and period of the Titanic's launch.**
   Both texts

6 **Text B gives an insight into a world where people of different social backgrounds were expected to behave differently. Find and write down two examples of this behaviour.**

   Sample answer:

   The narrator tells McKinlay to forget his orders to lock the cabin door which demonstrates that the first-class passengers could influence the staff on the ship more easily. This contrasts with below decks, where third-class passengers were being forced to remain on the sinking ship by the crew.

Early Bird: Word ladder (page 141)

> **Changing just one letter at a time, get from the word SEED to the word GROW in five steps.**
> SEED, SLED, SLEW, SLOW, GLOW, GROW